THIS BOOK BELONGS TO:

TO FOUR GENERATIONS OF NUOVO DRUMMERS... SO FAR
— A.N.

FOR JULIET
— D.D.

Orchestra is © Flying Eye Books 2019
First edition published in 2019 by Flying Eye Books, an imprint
of Nobrow Ltd. 27 Westgate Street, London, E8 3RL.

Text © Avalon Nuovo 2019
Illustrations © David Doran 2019

Consultant: Issie Barratt

Avalon Nuovo has asserted her right under the Copyright, Designs and Patents Act 1988, to be identified as the Author of this Work. David Doran has asserted his right under the Copyright, Designs and Patents Act, 1988, to be identified as the Illustrator of this Work.

All rights reserved. No part of this publication may be reproduced or transmitted in any form or by any means, electronic or mechanical, including photocopying, recording or by any information and storage retrieval system, without prior written consent from the publisher.

Every attempt has been made to ensure any statements written as fact have been checked to the best of our abilities. However, we are still human, thankfully, and occasionally little mistakes may crop up. Should you spot any errors, please email info@nobrow.net.

1 3 5 7 9 8 6 4 2

Published in the US by Nobrow (US) Inc.
Printed in Poland on FSC® certified paper

ISBN: 978-1-911171-20-1
www.flyingeyebooks.com

AVALON NUOVO • DAVID DORAN

ORCHESTRA

FLYING EYE BOOKS

LONDON • NEW YORK

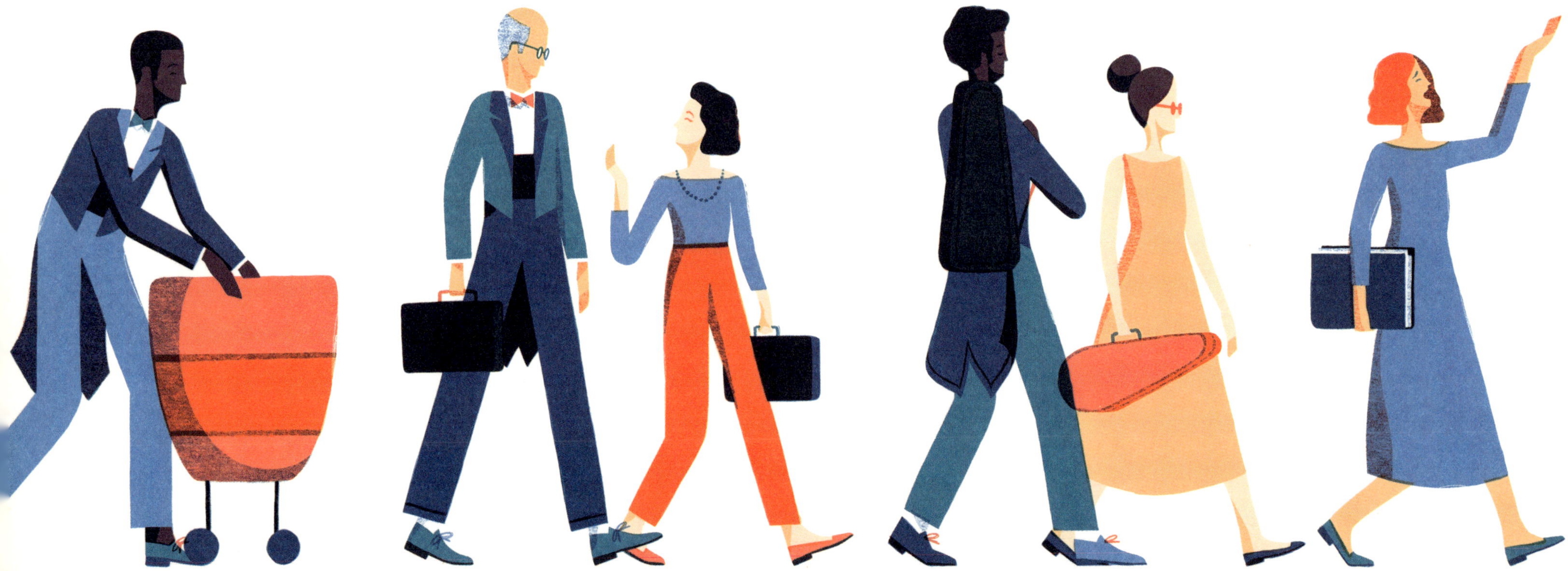

TABLE OF CONTENTS

THE ORCHESTRA

- 10 The Players and Their Stage
- 12 The Arrangement of an Orchestra
- 14 The String Section
- 16 How It Works: The Violin
- 18 The Woodwind Section
- 20 How It Works: The Clarinet
- 22 The Brass Section
- 24 How It Works: The Trumpet
- 26 The Percussion Section
- 28 How It Works: Percussion
- 30 Occasional Guests
- 32 You Are an Instrument, Too!
- 34 A Forest of Sound
- 36 How It Works: Concert Hall Acoustics
- 38 The Concert Hall: Wiener Musikverein

THE MUSIC AND ITS MAKERS

- 42 Reading Music
- 44 Composing the Music
- 46 Medieval Genius: Hildegard of Bingen
- 48 *The Four Seasons*: Antonio Vivaldi
- 50 Composition Pioneer: Amy Beach
- 52 *The Planets*: Gustav Holst
- 54 Big Band Maestro: Duke Ellington
- 56 Hall of Fame

BEYOND THE CONCERT HALL

- 60 Mythology of Music
- 62 Opera
- 64 Orchestra and Dance
- 66 Composing for Musical Theatre
- 68 Composing for Cinema
- 70 Orchestra and Technology
- 72 Getting Involved
- 74 Glossary
- 76 Index

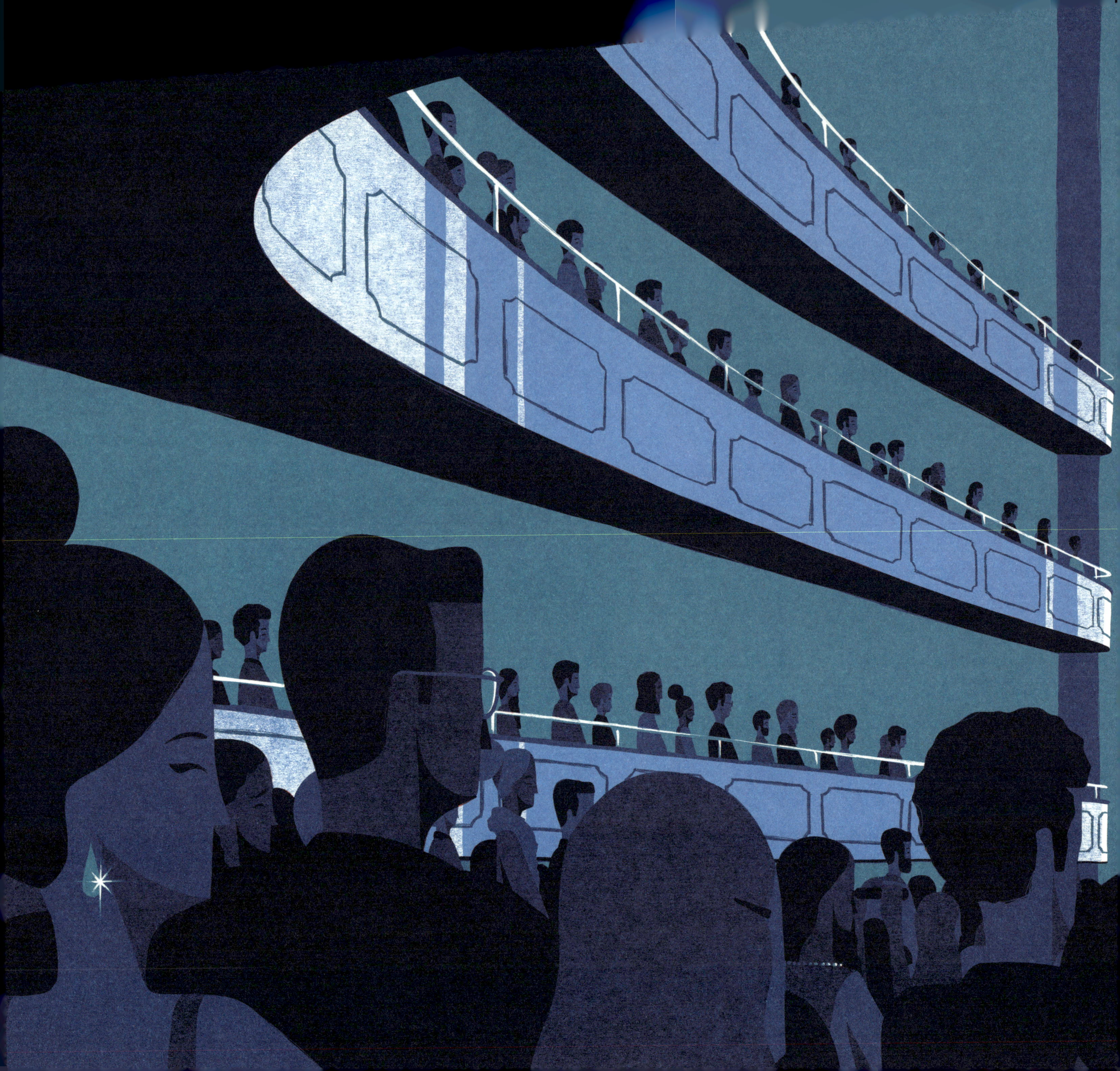

THE ORCHESTRA

THE PLAYERS AND THEIR STAGE

People have always made music. What started as a form of communication among indigenous groups around the world, eventually ended up as a way of entertaining onlookers and telling stories. People with a talent for music began forming groups to sing and play together, adding emotion and their own ideas to the mix. Different regions and groups created their own traditional melodies, as well as their own types of instruments.

Early versions of many western orchestral instruments we know today, such as the violin, the trumpet or the piano, were developed around six hundred years ago during a period in European history called the Renaissance. At this time, groups of musicians called **consorts** would play popular **melodies** with whichever instruments they had.

It wasn't until about two hundred years later that people started to compose music with specific instruments in mind. As groups of musicians grew bigger, different types of instruments were organised into sections. Each section played a part that was written specifically for it, and when all of these parts were played together… the first modern orchestra was born!

THE ARRANGEMENT OF AN ORCHESTRA

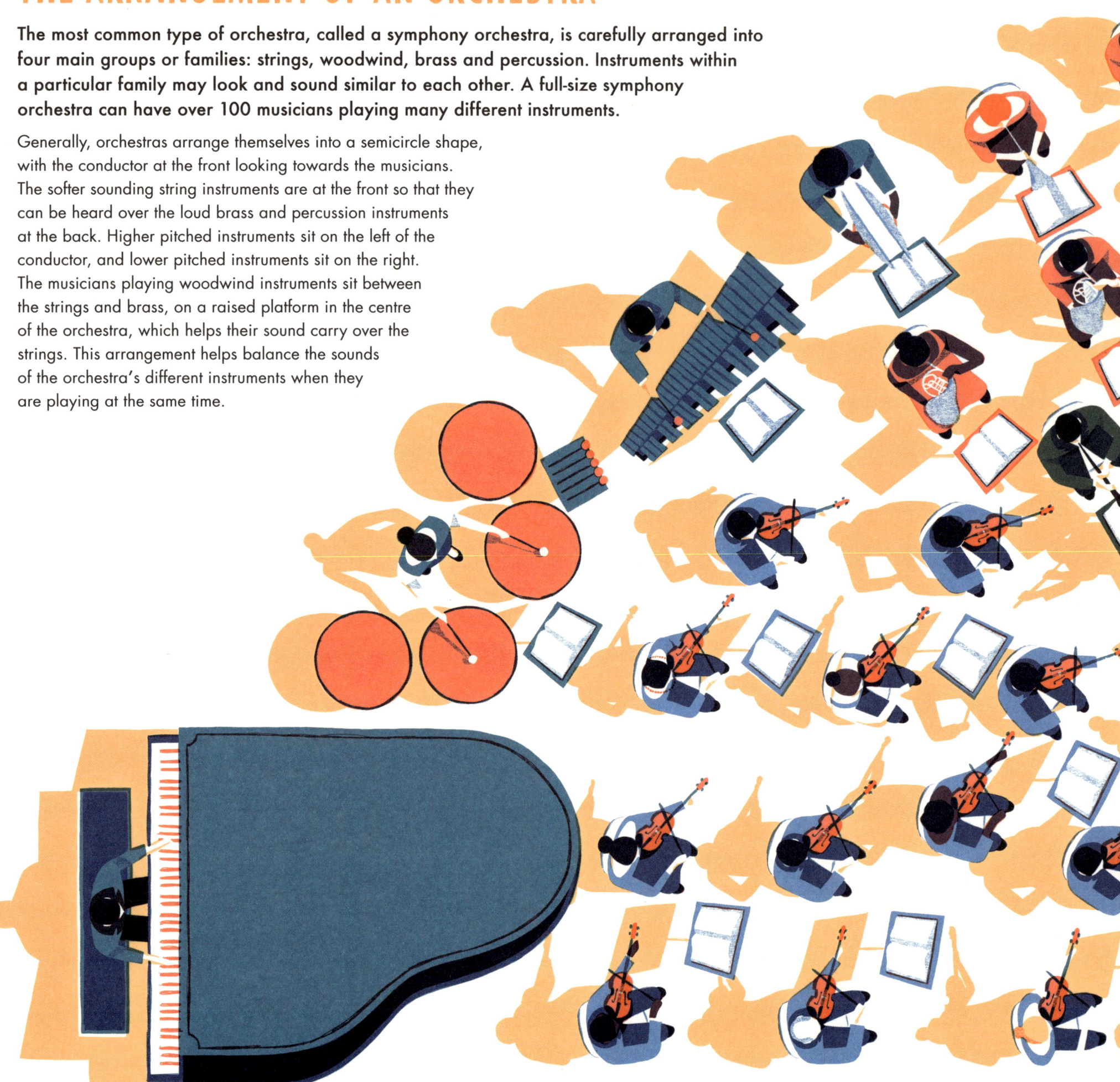

The most common type of orchestra, called a symphony orchestra, is carefully arranged into four main groups or families: strings, woodwind, brass and percussion. Instruments within a particular family may look and sound similar to each other. A full-size symphony orchestra can have over 100 musicians playing many different instruments.

Generally, orchestras arrange themselves into a semicircle shape, with the conductor at the front looking towards the musicians. The softer sounding string instruments are at the front so that they can be heard over the loud brass and percussion instruments at the back. Higher pitched instruments sit on the left of the conductor, and lower pitched instruments sit on the right. The musicians playing woodwind instruments sit between the strings and brass, on a raised platform in the centre of the orchestra, which helps their sound carry over the strings. This arrangement helps balance the sounds of the orchestra's different instruments when they are playing at the same time.

CONDUCTOR

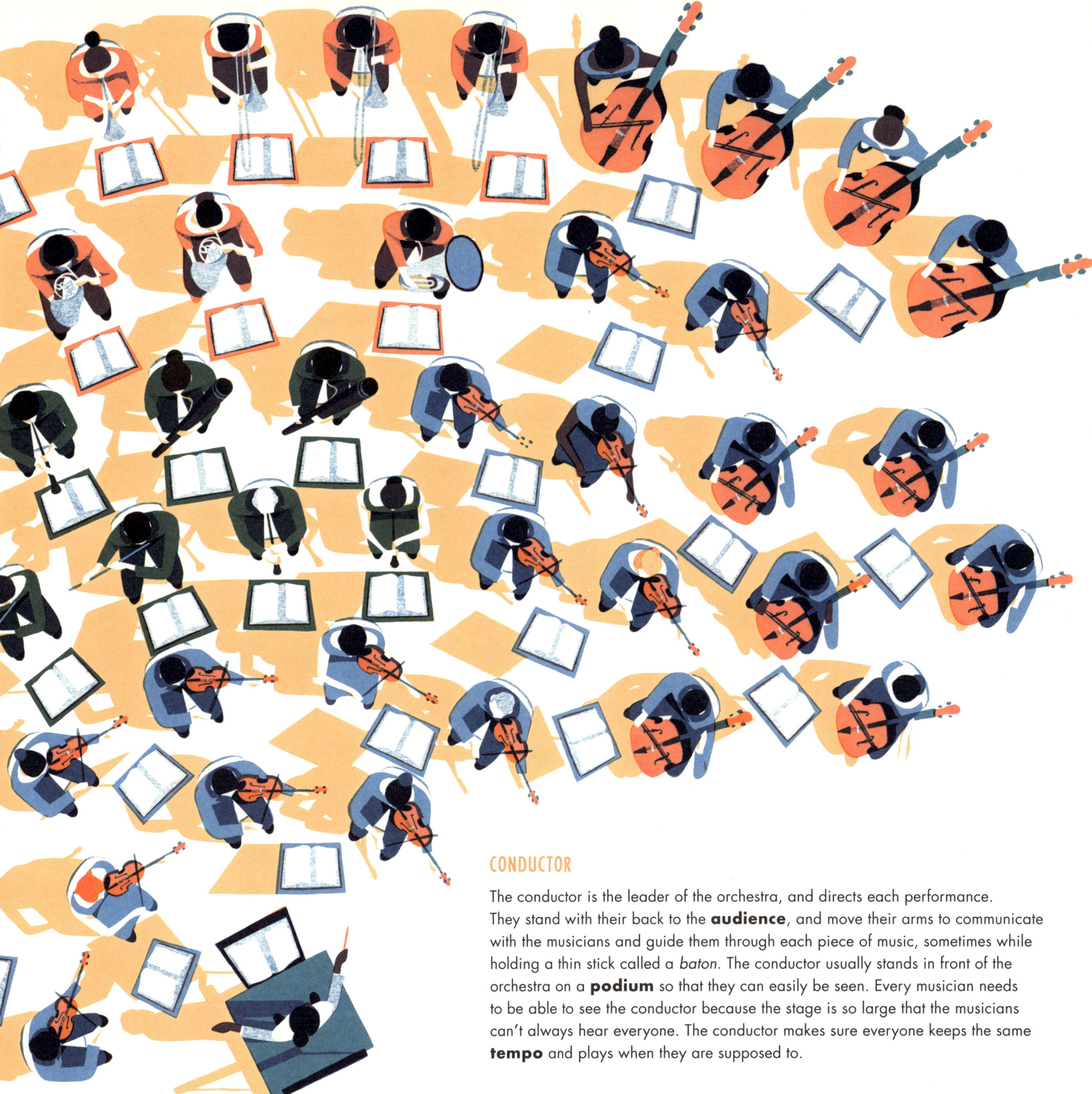

The conductor is the leader of the orchestra, and directs each performance. They stand with their back to the **audience**, and move their arms to communicate with the musicians and guide them through each piece of music, sometimes while holding a thin stick called a *baton*. The conductor usually stands in front of the orchestra on a **podium** so that they can easily be seen. Every musician needs to be able to see the conductor because the stage is so large that the musicians can't always hear everyone. The conductor makes sure everyone keeps the same **tempo** and plays when they are supposed to.

THE STRING SECTION

String instruments are usually made of wood, but the part that produces the sound is their strings. Each instrument has four strings, which can be played by drawing the hairs of a bow across them, plucking them with a musicians' fingers or striking them with the wooden side of a bow. Most players use their right hand to move the bow. They use their left hand to control what **note** is played by holding down the instrument's strings in different places along its neck.

VIOLA

The violas usually play **accompaniments** and harmonies. A viola has a deeper sound than a violin because it is bigger, and its thicker, heavier strings require a larger bow to play. It has a higher sound than a cello, and so is normally positioned at the heart of the orchestra – the middle.

VIOLIN

Violins are the smallest instruments in the orchestra's string family and have the highest **pitch**. There are two types: first violins, which usually play the melodies, and second violins, which play **harmonies** or accompanying parts. The first and second violins sit in pairs. The leader (or principal) of the first violins sits at the front and also leads the whole orchestra.

CELLO

The cello looks a lot like a violin or viola, but it is much bigger, has a deeper sound and plays with a lower pitch. Due to its size, the cellist must rest it on the floor using a spike, and hold it upright in order to play.

DOUBLE BASS

The largest instrument in the string family is the double bass, also known simply as the bass. With a very low pitch and a rich sound, the double bass is so enormous that it is taller than many of the musicians who play it!

CHIN REST

The chin rest helps the violinist position their instrument comfortably under their chin.

TAILPIECE

The tailpiece holds the strings onto the instrument.

BRIDGE

This piece keeps the four strings in position and carries their vibrations to the body of the violin, **amplifying** their sound.

BODY

The violin's body is made from wood. The top, called the **soundboard**, is made of softer wood, so that it can better transfer sound vibrations.

HOW IT WORKS: THE VIOLIN

Each stringed instrument has a number of components that piece together like a puzzle. Instruments in the violin family come in different sizes and have slightly different shapes, but they are built in a similar way. Let's take a closer look at a violin to see how it works.

BOW

This a long piece of wood, with a ribbon of horse hair or plastic thread pulled tight between its two ends. Musicians regularly apply **rosin** to their bow hairs. This increases their friction against the strings, which is what produces the sound.

SOUND HOLES

The sound holes (called *f-holes* due to their shape) allow the soundboard to **vibrate**, and also let **sound waves** travel out of the instrument.

SOUND POST

This small wooden post inside the violin makes the instrument more sturdy and helps its sound to **resonate**.

STRINGS

Some violin strings are made of sheep intestines, while others are made of plastic or metal. When the musician presses the string down onto the fingerboard with their left hand, this changes the pitch that the string makes when plucked or bowed with the right hand.

NECK AND FINGERBOARD

The flat part of the neck which faces upward is called the fingerboard. This is where the musician places their fingers in order to change the notes. The thumb is used to balance the instrument by placing it under the neck.

PEGBOX

The pegbox contains one peg for each of the violin's four strings. Turning each peg tightens or loosens its string, which is how the instrument is **tuned**.

SCROLL

This decorative piece is carved to look like a scroll of paper.

THE WOODWIND SECTION

Once only made from wood, today these instruments might also use metal, plastic, or a combination of materials. It is the musicians' breath that creates the 'wind' of the woodwind section as they blow into their instruments.

FLUTE

The flute is a high-pitched instrument with a very light, floaty sound. Professionals use flutes made of solid silver, gold, and sometimes platinum, but beginners will use flutes made of nickel or brass that are silver-plated as they are lighter.

OBOE

The conical shape of the inside of this instrument means that it has a very strong, clear sound, which can easily be heard amongst the orchestra. This, in addition to the fact that it stays in tune more consistently than string instruments, is the reason why the entire orchestra tunes their instrument to the oboe.

CLARINET

Clarinets come in many shapes and sizes, from the tiny sopranino clarinet to the enormous contrabass clarinet, which can play notes even lower than the double bass! Often used for romantic melodies, the clarinet's clear sound can be played both very loud and surprisingly soft.

BASSOON

The bassoon has the lowest pitch of the woodwind family. It is extremely versatile, which means players can produce both very low and very high notes. It produces a sound that many say sounds a lot like a low human voice.

HOW IT WORKS: THE CLARINET

If you see a woodwind instrument in small pieces, don't worry – it's not broken! They are meant to be simple to assemble and disassemble, which makes them easier to clean and carry around. Woodwind instruments are all built in a similar way. Take a look at this clarinet to learn more about how they work.

Most instruments in the woodwind family are called reed instruments. The reed is what gives reed instruments their name. Some instruments, like the oboe or the bassoon, have two reeds that vibrate against each other. These are called double reed instruments. Their mouthpieces look like this.

UPPER JOINT
The top half of the instrument body, this contains the keys for the left hand.

There is one woodwind instrument which doesn't have a reed at all: the flute. The **flautist** must blow air across the hole in its mouthpiece instead. This is why flautists hold their instruments sideways, unlike other woodwind players.

LOWER JOINT
The bottom half of the instrument body, this contains the keys for the right hand.

BELL
This is the end where the sound comes out of the instrument. Its conical shape helps to amplify sound.

REED

The reed is made of a type of plant, which is similar to grass or bamboo. When the player blows into the instrument, it is the reed's vibration against the mouthpiece that makes the sound. The clarinet has a single reed.

MOUTHPIECE

This is the very top of the clarinet, where the player blows air to produce sound.

LIGATURE

This small piece of metal holds the reed firmly in place on the mouthpiece.

BARREL

This connects the mouthpiece with the instrument body, and helps carry sound.

REGISTER KEY

This key, played by the musician's thumb, raises or lowers the pitch so that it can play a greater range of notes.

KEYS

This is where the player places their fingers. Each key lifts or lowers little caps onto the holes of the instrument, changing the pitch of the sound it makes. The more fingers added, the lower the note.

THE BRASS SECTION

Similar to woodwinds, these instruments are brought to life by a musician's breath. However, they have a much louder, more powerful sound. These energetic instruments are often part of the signature sound of jazz bands. There are many different brass instruments that can be used in an orchestra, but the ones you see here are the most common.

FRENCH HORN

The French horn is a versatile instrument. Capable of producing a wide range of sounds, it can make both loud and harsh noises as well as quiet and soft ones. In an orchestra, French horns play the main melodies and harmonies.

TRUMPET

The trumpet is the smallest brass instrument and has the highest pitch. It is made from a long piece of brass tubing that has been wound twice into a rounded oblong shape. It might be small, but if its tube were unwound and laid out straight, it would be nearly two metres long!

TUBA

The tuba is the largest instrument in the brass family, and has the lowest pitch. The concert tuba is shown here, but you might recognise the sousaphone, too – a type of tuba that wraps around the player so that they can play while marching in a band.

TROMBONE

A trombone is made by two U-shaped pipes that are linked together to form an 'S' shape. It is great fun to watch a trombonist move the slide back and forth with their right hand as they play! When played as loudly as possible, the trombone is louder than any other instrument in a traditional orchestra.

HOW IT WORKS: THE TRUMPET

Remember how woodwind players use a vibrating reed to produce sound? Brass instruments have no reeds, so the musician has to blow air through pursed lips, causing the air inside the instrument to vibrate. This technique is called **embouchure**. Most brass instruments, like this trumpet, use a series of **valves** to change their pitch. A closer look at this trumpet will show us how this works.

TUBES

The trombone does not use valves like the others. Instead, the player moves a large tube back and forth, which lengthens or shortens the instrument's tubing and changes the pitch.

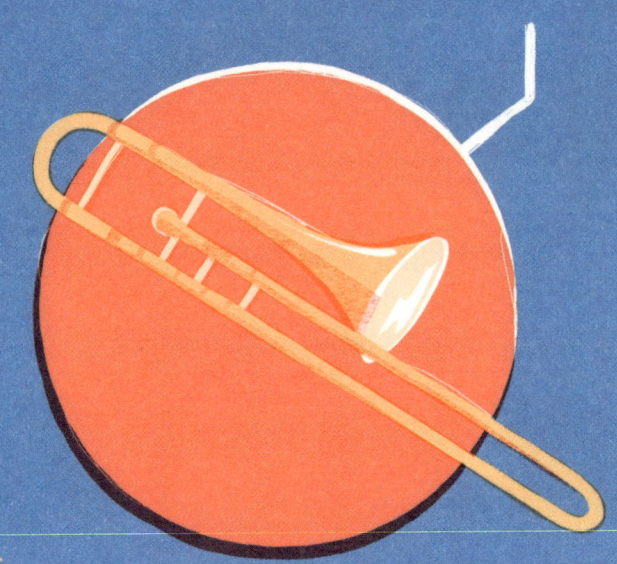

MUTE

Because brass instruments are so powerful, their players can also use a mute to make the instrument quieter or to change its sound. This is placed inside the bell. There are four main types of mute, and each one does something a bit different. The Harmon mute for example, creates a 'wah-wah' sound.

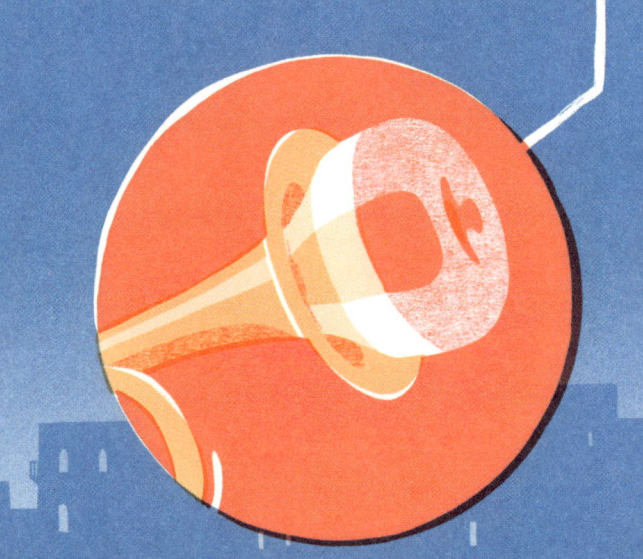

MOUTHPIECE

This is where the musician blows into the instrument. Its shape helps to amplify the vibrations created by the trumpeter's lips.

VALVE PISTONS

The musician raises or lowers these three pistons with their fingers to control how their breath moves through the trumpet. When air is forced to move differently by these pistons, it changes the pitch, allowing the trumpeter to choose what note to play.

BELL

The bell is where sound emerges from the instrument, and its shape helps to amplify its sound.

TUNING SLIDE

Similar to valve slides but a bit longer, the tuning slide also helps to change the pitch of the trumpet.

FINGER HOOKS

These sturdy metal loops give the trumpeter a way to grip the instrument while they play.

VALVE CASINGS

These tubes hold the valve pistons.

VALVE SLIDES

These three pieces of tubing can be moved in and out to help tune the instrument or change its pitch.

THE PERCUSSION SECTION

Crashing, striking, shaking – these instruments keep the **rhythm** and bring energy to performances. A **percussionist** will often play many different instruments during one performance. Within this large section, there are two smaller groups: tuned percussion and untuned percussion.

TUNED PERCUSSION

This group can play melodies, because they can strike different parts of their instrument to play different notes.

XYLOPHONE

The xylophone has a row of wooden keys which are arranged like the keys of a piano, and is played by striking the keys with a special mallet. There are many different types of xylophone. They come in different sizes and have keys made of different materials, including the metal vibraphone and the wooden marimba. These materials all give a distinct sound.

TIMPANI

The timpani, also called a kettledrum, is a type of drum made by stretching animal skin or plastic over the opening of a large bowl, which is usually made from copper. Most orchestras have four timpani, all played by one musician.

PIANO

The piano is often used in the orchestra to accompany percussion or add more **texture**, but it can also be played as a solo instrument. During a piano solo, the pianist will play the melody with one hand and the harmony with the other. Foot-operated pedals can be used to enrich the sound, or soften it.

UNTUNED PERCUSSION

This group can play rhythms but not melodies, as their instruments can only produce one pitch. Among them are the bass drum, cymbals, snare drum and castanets.

Cymbals   Snare drum   Bass drum   Castanets

HOW IT WORKS: PERCUSSION

You may have started to see a pattern in how instruments work. Some use air, some are plucked or bowed, but all of them are doing the same thing to make sound: vibrating. With percussion, vibrations come from the force of the player striking the instrument. Here is a closer look at some of the percussion instruments we just learned about.

SNARE DRUM

Like the timpani, the drumhead of this instrument vibrates when the percussionist strikes it, causing vibrations which resonate inside the drum. It is played using drum sticks. The part of the snare drum that gives it its name is a series of coiled metal wires or strings which are attached to the bottom of it. They produce a sharp rattling sound when the drum is struck, giving the snare drum its unique sound.

Timpani

Snare drum

TIMPANI

When a percussionist strikes the drumhead of a timpani with a mallet, the vibrations resonate inside the shell or bowl of the drum, amplifying the sound. The pitch of a timpani can be adjusted by slightly tightening or loosening the skin of the drumhead. Old-style timpanis use a tuning bolt, but more modern timpanis have pedals that allow the player to adjust the tuning. This enables them to use a wider range of notes thoughout the piece.

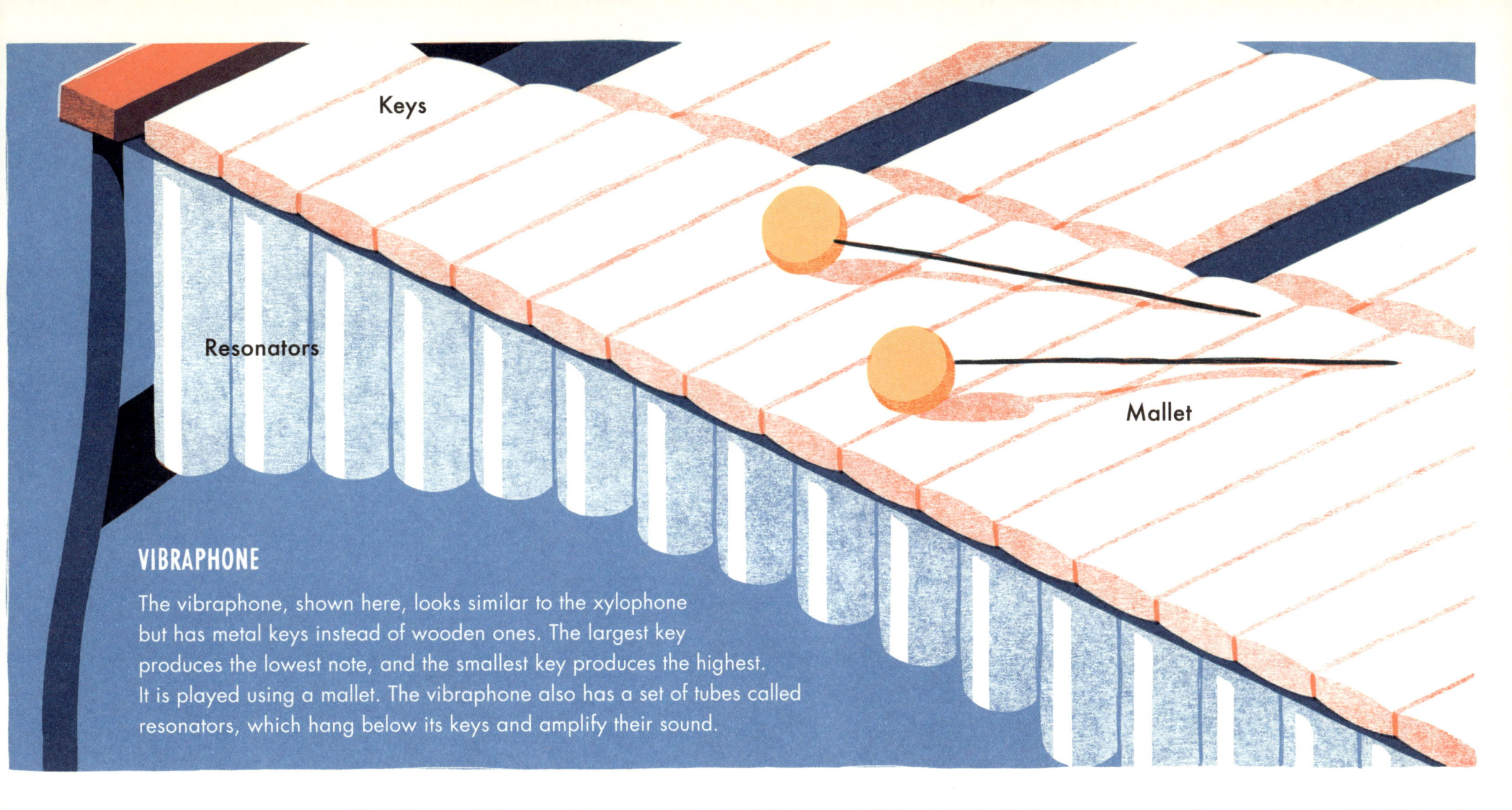

Keys

Resonators

Mallet

VIBRAPHONE

The vibraphone, shown here, looks similar to the xylophone but has metal keys instead of wooden ones. The largest key produces the lowest note, and the smallest key produces the highest. It is played using a mallet. The vibraphone also has a set of tubes called resonators, which hang below its keys and amplify their sound.

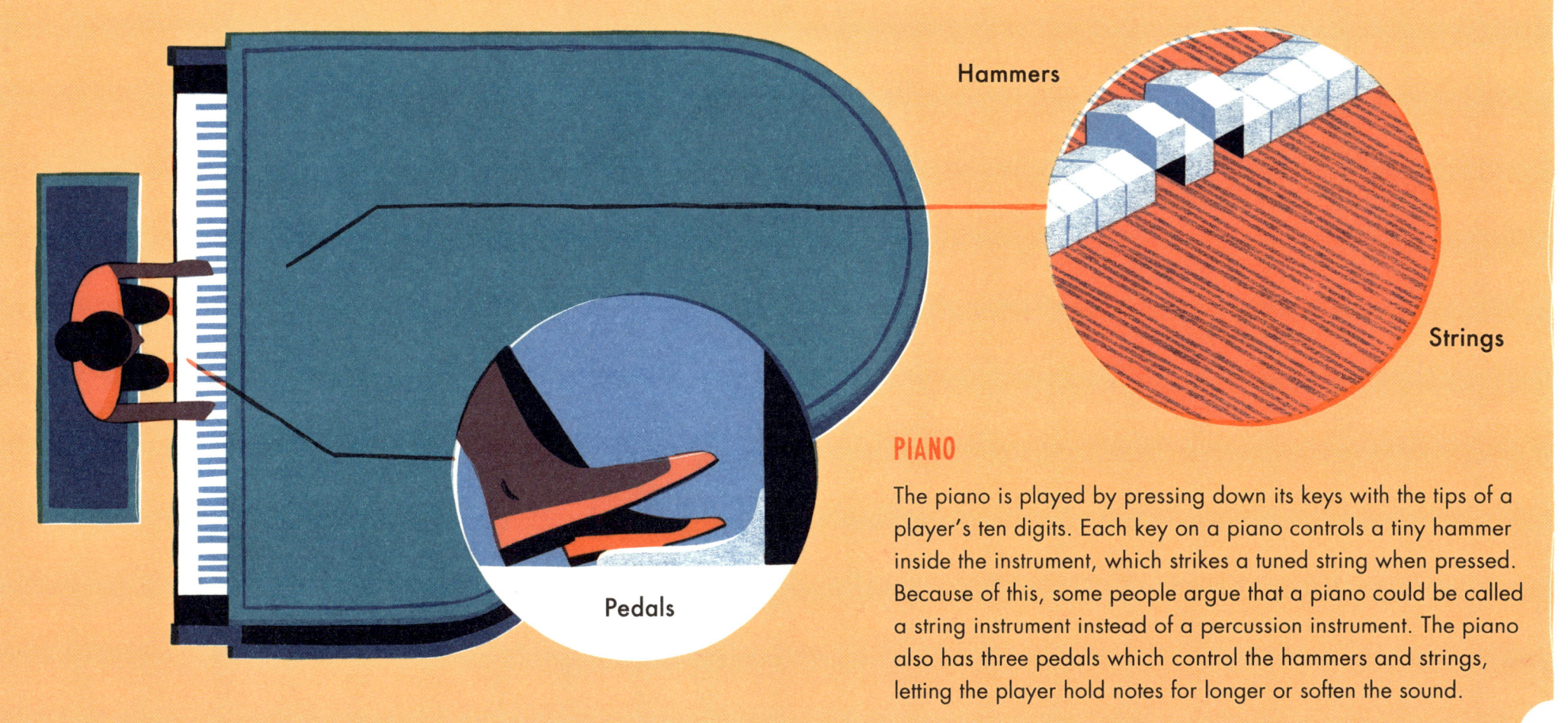

Hammers

Strings

Pedals

PIANO

The piano is played by pressing down its keys with the tips of a player's ten digits. Each key on a piano controls a tiny hammer inside the instrument, which strikes a tuned string when pressed. Because of this, some people argue that a piano could be called a string instrument instead of a percussion instrument. The piano also has three pedals which control the hammers and strings, letting the player hold notes for longer or soften the sound.

OCCASIONAL GUESTS

There are some instruments which don't always appear in a typical orchestra line-up. Let's take a look at some of these occasional guests.

HARP

The harp is one of the oldest stringed instruments in the world, and is known for its delicate, sweeping sound. A harpist plucks individual strings with their fingers.

ORGAN

There are many different types of organ, but the grandest is the pipe organ. This enormous instrument looks a bit like a piano with many keyboards – including one that is played using the performer's feet! Its sound is produced by air being pushed through a vast array of pipes. Different pipes have different sounds, and the organist can choose from these by pushing or pulling various levers. There are so many sounds and keys to choose from, that some organ keyboards can look like the cockpit of a spaceship, and often a second person is needed to help out!

CLASSICAL GUITAR

You've probably seen guitars in rock bands, but did you know they are used in orchestras as well? The guitar you see here is called a classical guitar. It is a type of acoustic guitar, which means that it doesn't use **electronics** to create sound the way that electric guitars do. Instead, the body is **hollow** with a hole in the centre, amplifying the sound. A guitarist plays the instrument by plucking its six strings with their fingers or a small piece of plastic called a *pick*, or *plectrum*.

SAXOPHONE

Despite being made of brass, the saxophone is a member of the woodwind family. This is because the sound is produced with a reed, just like the clarinet. The saxophone is rare in symphony orchestras and is more commonly found in jazz music.

YOU ARE AN INSTRUMENT, TOO!

There is one very important musical instrument that we haven't mentioned yet: your own voice! The vocal chords in your throat produce sound by vibrating as your breath passes between them, which is quite similar to the way wind instruments work. Like any other musician, a professional singer must spend years learning how to hold their body, breathe properly and form their mouth so that the sound they produce is clear, beautiful, projected and in tune.

Some orchestral pieces feature one or more performers singing their own (solo) part. These are called *soloists*. Other compositions call for a choir, which is a group of people who all sing a piece of music together. A choir is organised much like an orchestra. Each different section usually has its own part, so that when all of them are sung together they create harmony. When all of the groups are singing exactly the same thing, however, it is called **unison**.

Singers are arranged in sections according to their **vocal range**. In some choirs, this is organised so that the highest singers are at one end and the lowest singers are at the other.

Soprano (highest) Mezzo-soprano Contralto Tenor Countertenor Baritone Bass (lowest)

A FOREST OF SOUND

When it comes to wooden instruments, the type of tree that is used can make a big difference in the way an instrument sounds. In some cases, a single instrument can be made from a combination of different types of wood.

Maple

Ebony

Cocobolo

Pernambuco

HARDWOODS

Hardwoods are dense, meaning that they are very strong and durable. This makes them great for the sides, back, neck and pegbox of stringed instruments, which need to be able to support the strong tension of the strings. Ebony is an example of a hardwood tree. This dark-coloured wood is often used for violin and viola chin rests and fingerboards, or the black keys of the piano, because it is durable enough to withstand years of repeated pressure as well as oil from the player's skin

Cedar

Spruce

SOFTWOODS

Softwood trees are more **porous** and flexible than hardwoods, which means they are better for transferring sound vibrations. This makes them perfect for the soundboard of stringed instruments such as the violin or guitar. Before it can be used, the wood is first dried to remove the moisture, making it less likely to bend and split later. Lightweight spruces are known to provide a rich, clear tone for acoustic guitars.

HOW IT WORKS: CONCERT HALL ACOUSTICS

Just like the best place to hear a play is the theatre, the best place to hear orchestral music is a concert hall. This is a special type of theatre that is built especially for musical performances. A concert hall is carefully designed so that the music played inside it will sound as wonderful as possible.

The very best concert halls mix together science, **engineering** and art. Architects make sure that these grand halls are beautiful, inspiring places that are as brilliant as the music that is performed within them. However, there is a lot more to a concert hall than its appearance. Its shape, the angles of its walls, and the placement of columns and seats are all architectural features which can change the way music sounds within a hall. Engineers and scientists who know a great deal about **acoustics** work very hard to ensure that everything in a concert hall is built in just the right way.

Sydney Opera House, Australia

Elbphilharmonie, Germany

Royal Albert Hall, England

THE CONCERT HALL:
WIENER MUSIKVEREIN

According to most experts in acoustics, the concert hall with the greatest sound quality in the world is the Wiener Musikverein in Vienna, Austria. It was designed by Danish architect Theophil Hansen, and was completed in the year 1870.

Today, scientists and engineers know a great deal about acoustics, so they can use mathematical formulas to figure out how sound will travel inside a concert hall before it is even built. However, at the time when Musikverein was designed, there were no studies on acoustics. The brilliant acoustics of the hall are simply due to Hansen's excellent understanding of the way sound works. The Great Hall's shoebox shape and proportions, its boxes and sculptures – allow sound to reflect in a way that makes music sound incredible.

39

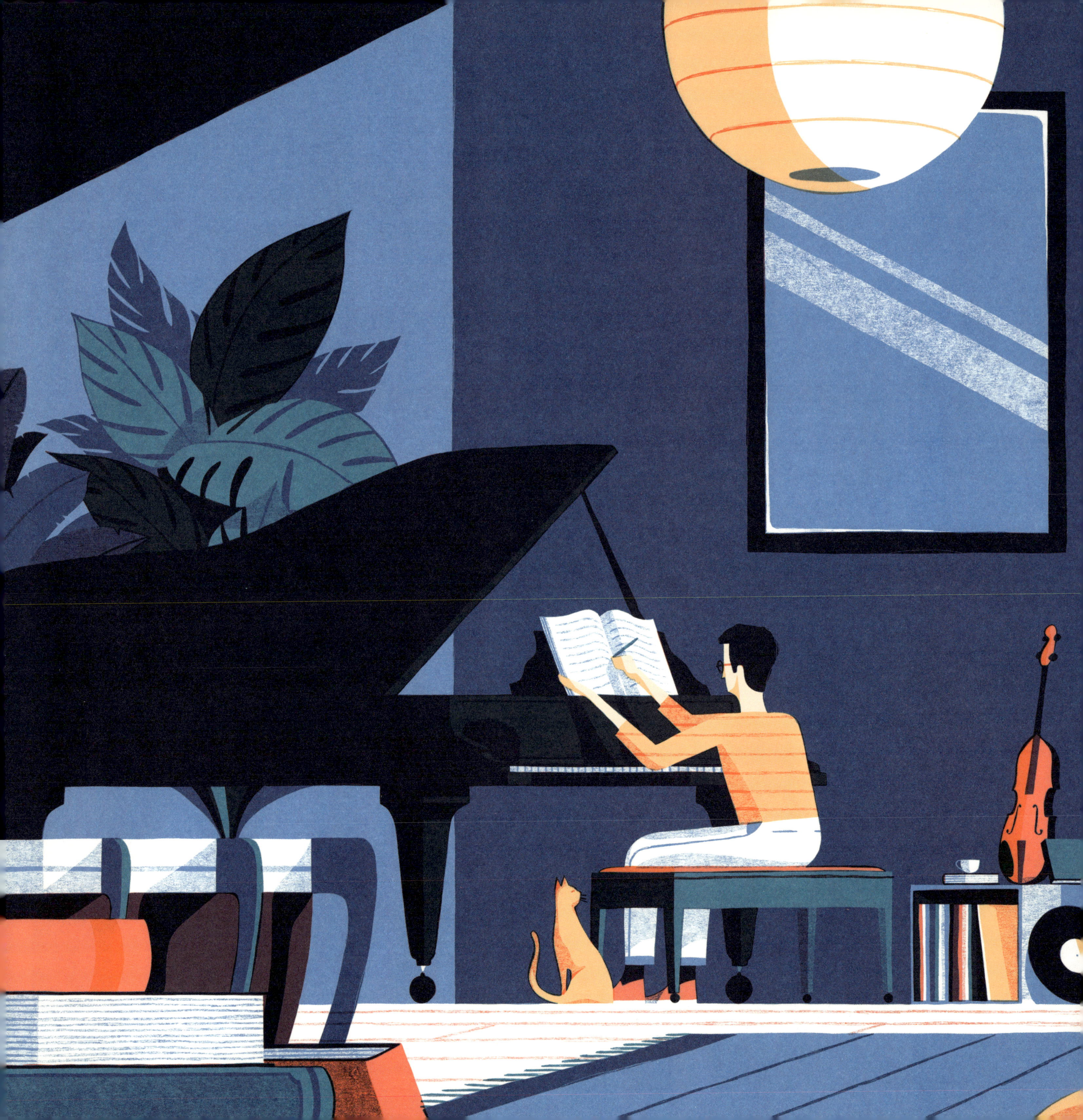

THE MUSIC AND ITS MAKERS

READING MUSIC

How do the musicians in an orchestra know what to play and when to play it? While they perform, they are actually reading the music, much in the same way you might read aloud from a book. It is possible to **memorise** a piece of music with a lot of practice, but professional musicians know how to **sight-read**, meaning that they are able to play a piece of music that they have never seen before just by reading it.

Written music uses a stave. This is a series of five lines that go across the page. Each line, and each space between lines, represents a different note, and we refer to these notes by giving each of them a letter of the alphabet from A to G. When a note symbol is placed on a line or a space in the stave, it tells the musician which note to play.

This symbol is called a *clef*. It sits at the beginning of the stave, and indicates the pitch the notes are to be played in.

Not all notes are created equal! Music frequently relies on regular beats which are often grouped together. For example, two beats are commonly used in a march rhythm, while four beats are often used in pop music. Written music tells musicians what notes to play, but it also tells them when to play it, and how fast. Different symbols tell the player how long to hold each note. In the diagram on the right, each note is twice as long as the note to its left. The quaver for example is very quick, whereas the semibreve is held for much longer.

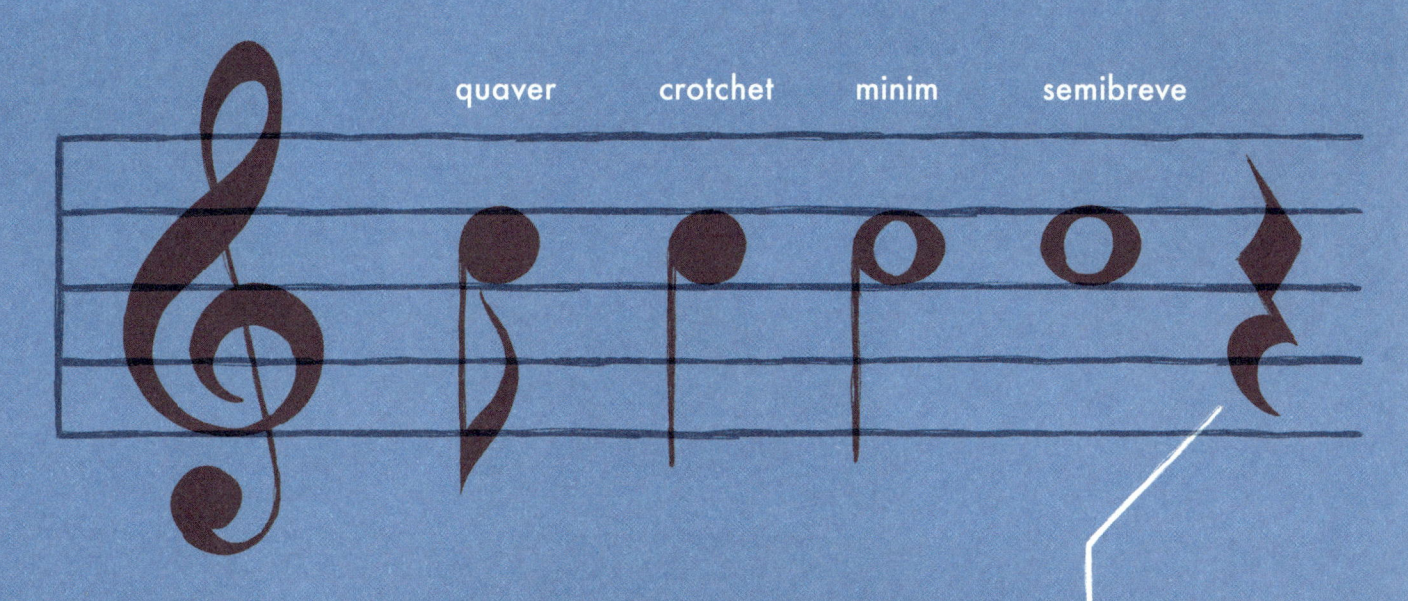

quaver   crotchet   minim   semibreve

This special symbol is called a *rest*. It means that for this **beat**, the musician should play nothing at all!

43

COMPOSING THE MUSIC

The person who writes the music played by an orchestra is called a composer, and a piece of music that is written for an orchestra is usually called a symphony or a concerto.

A composer has many things to consider. They create the melody of the song, arrange harmonies and decide the tempo and rhythm that will carry the music along. The composer also chooses which instruments will play each part of the music. Often, each instrument will play only part of the time during a performance. The composer chooses when each instrument will play, and when it will rest, so that they can control the sound and **dynamics**. In a play, all the actors can read each other's parts from a script, but in an orchestra, a musician only reads the part they are going to play. The conductor is the only person to have a copy of what all the instruments are playing together – this is called the *score*.

forte / loud

The choices a composer makes when writing music are all meant to help them tell a story. A good composer knows how to arrange music so that their audience feels a certain emotion or imagines a certain scene. One of the wonderful things about orchestral music is that because it usually does not have **lyrics**, it can be understood by anyone in the world, no matter what language they speak. A composer can write music about anything that inspires them. If you were to write a piece of music, which story would you tell?

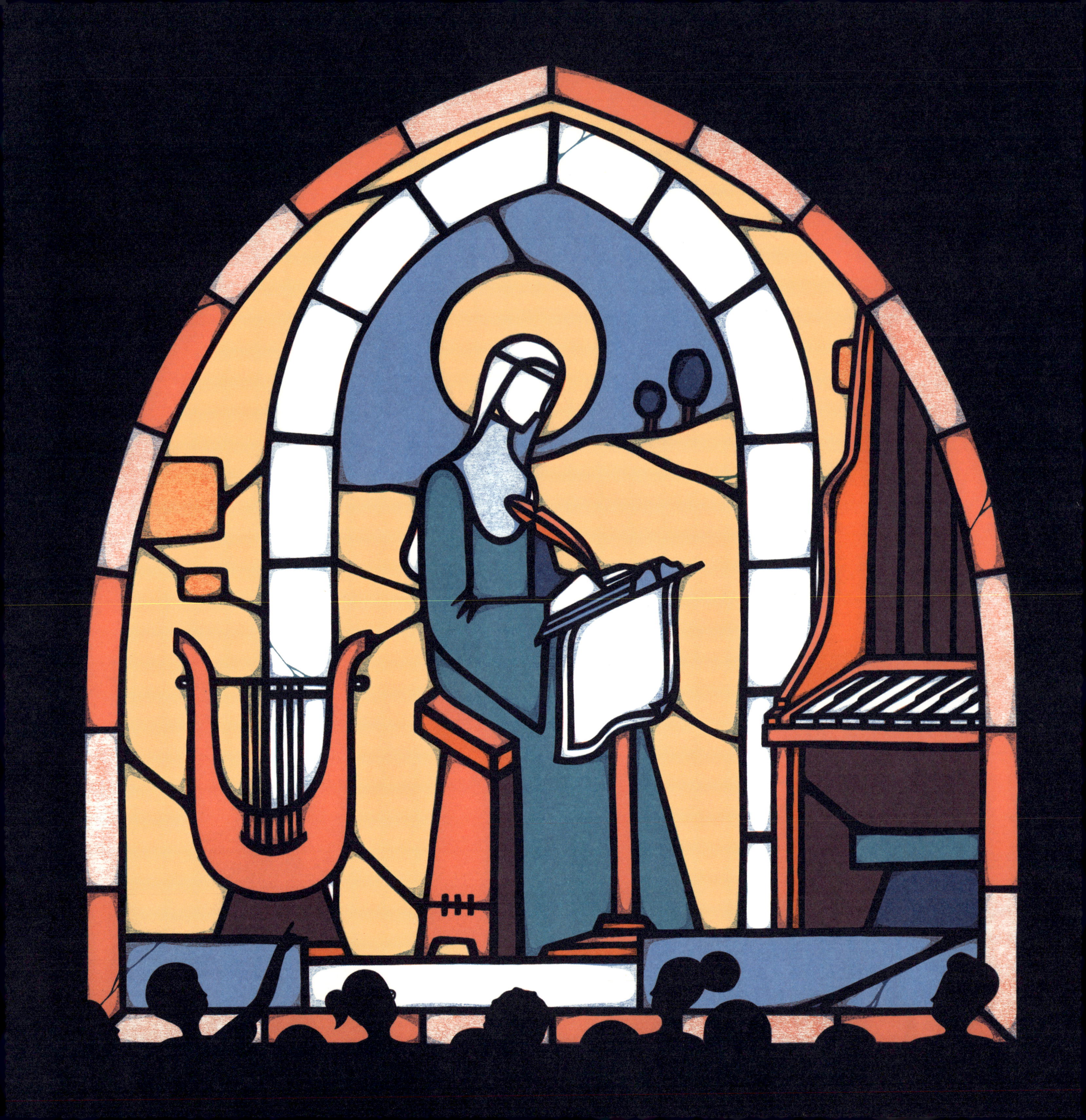

MEDIEVAL GENIUS:
HILDEGARD OF BINGEN
(1098–1179)

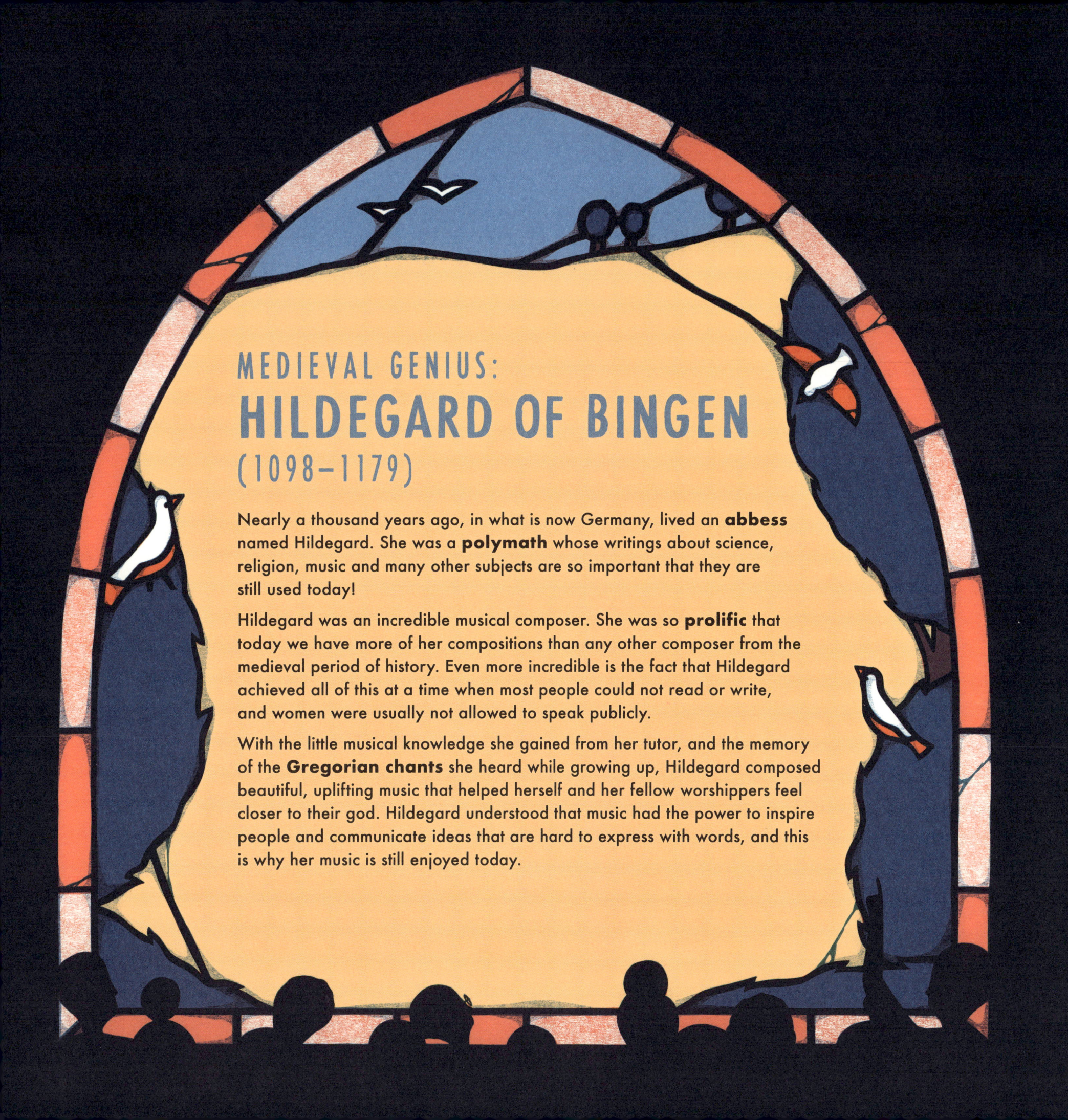

Nearly a thousand years ago, in what is now Germany, lived an **abbess** named Hildegard. She was a **polymath** whose writings about science, religion, music and many other subjects are so important that they are still used today!

Hildegard was an incredible musical composer. She was so **prolific** that today we have more of her compositions than any other composer from the medieval period of history. Even more incredible is the fact that Hildegard achieved all of this at a time when most people could not read or write, and women were usually not allowed to speak publicly.

With the little musical knowledge she gained from her tutor, and the memory of the **Gregorian chants** she heard while growing up, Hildegard composed beautiful, uplifting music that helped herself and her fellow worshippers feel closer to their god. Hildegard understood that music had the power to inspire people and communicate ideas that are hard to express with words, and this is why her music is still enjoyed today.

THE FOUR SEASONS (LE QUATTRO STAGIONI)
ANTONIO VIVALDI (1678–1741)

Antonio Vivaldi was an Italian composer, **virtuoso** violinist and teacher. Vivaldi's most well-known work is his series of concertos called *The Four Seasons*. Each concerto has three **movements**, and tells the story of one of the four seasons of the year. These concertos are still so popular that you might even have heard some of them already without realising it!

SPRING

In this first movement, violins imitate cheerful bird songs and water bubbling across a small stream. The beautiful spring day builds into a thunderstorm of ominous, frenzied violins. When the storm passes, the steady, peaceful melodies of the second movement describe a goat herder sleeping in a field with his dog at his side. The third movement bursts with energy as nymphs and shepherds dance together amongst happy violins and a joyful melody.

SUMMER

This concerto begins slowly and lazily like the intense heat of a summer's day, with the deep sounds of a brewing storm. The shepherd is hard at work with the sun beating down on him. As the storm tries to break, the music grows more and more intense, until it bursts into a hurried and lively song as the storm takes hold: thunder, wind and rain overwhelm the shepherd!

AUTUMN

Autumn opens as peasants sing and dance with great energy, until the quieter second movement brings cool autumn wind and the peasants ready themselves for sleep. The third movement brings the energy of a great hunt, with horns blowing as hunters ride out on horseback and dogs chase at their heels.

WINTER

A higher pitch and quickened tempo describe the danger of stinging winds and biting cold. With an ominous feel, the three movements weave together in a gentle rhythm that breaks sharply and quickens into dramatic, icy **climaxes**.

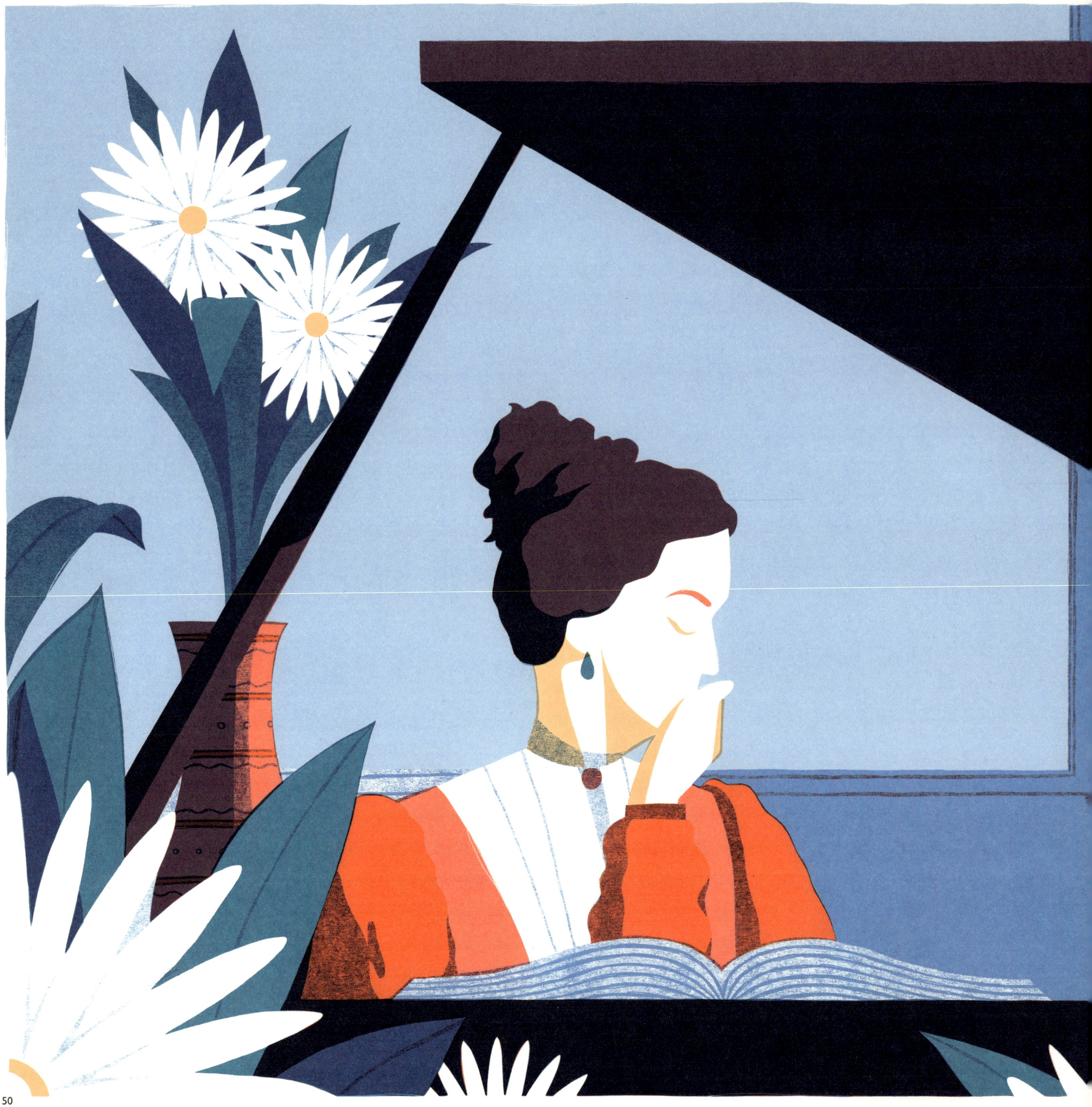

COMPOSITION PIONEER:
AMY BEACH
(1867–1944)

Even a hundred years ago, many people still believed that women were not able to compose symphonies simply because they were women. Amy Beach proved this wrong in 1896, when her *Gaelic Symphony* was first performed with tremendous success. It was the first symphony ever written by an American woman, and it made her a true **pioneer** in music and women's rights.

The *Gaelic Symphony* swells and floats with energy and emotion, creating a grand musical piece that is woven with traditional Irish folk melodies. When it premiered in Boston, U.S., to a room full of journalists and critics, it was immediately met with high acclaim, and it went on to be performed across the world.

THE PLANETS
GUSTAV HOLST (1874–1934)

Gustav Holst was an English composer, teacher and professional trombonist. His most well-known work was *The Planets*, an orchestral **suite** that was inspired by his interest in astronomy. Each movement of the suite describes the character of one of the planets in our solar system.

MARS: THE BRINGER OF WAR

A drum beat marches through this piece, giving a strong military feeling. Holst captured the anger and roughness of fiery Mars with a pulsing rhythm and orchestral climaxes.

VENUS: THE BRINGER OF PEACE

Venus is a slow and peaceful movement. With soft flutes and shimmering strings, it is eerie and almost romantic in its sound.

MERCURY: THE WINGED MESSENGER

A quickened tempo and a high-pitched harp, flute and glockenspiel create a sense of lightness and speed.

JUPITER: THE BRINGER OF JOY

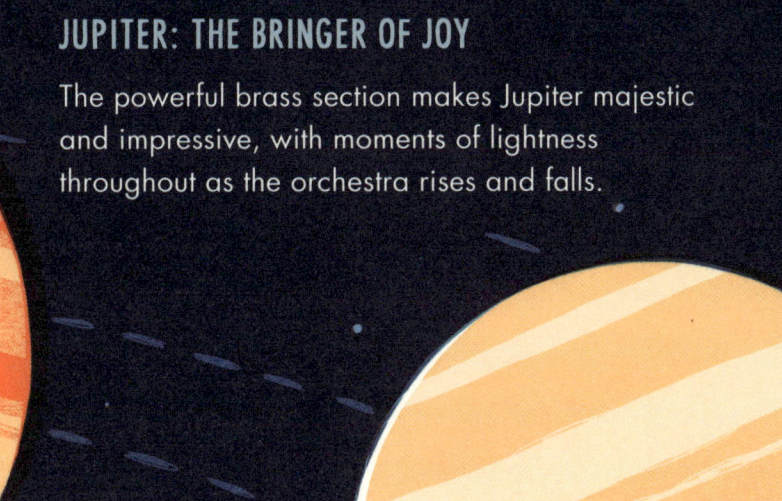

The powerful brass section makes Jupiter majestic and impressive, with moments of lightness throughout as the orchestra rises and falls.

SATURN: THE BRINGER OF OLD AGE

Saturn's unsettling opening builds into a slow and steady march that is meant to feel like the ceaseless pace of time.

URANUS: THE MAGICIAN

Starting with four strong brassy notes, Uranus moves from bold timpani blows to an energetic roll of percussion. The full orchestra conveys the sheer power of the planet in this grand, **uptempo** movement.

NEPTUNE: THE MYSTIC

The sound of an organ gives this movement a sense of deep mystery. Sometimes chaotic, sometimes layered with beautiful harp and string melodies, this movement ends with an ethereal-sounding choir.

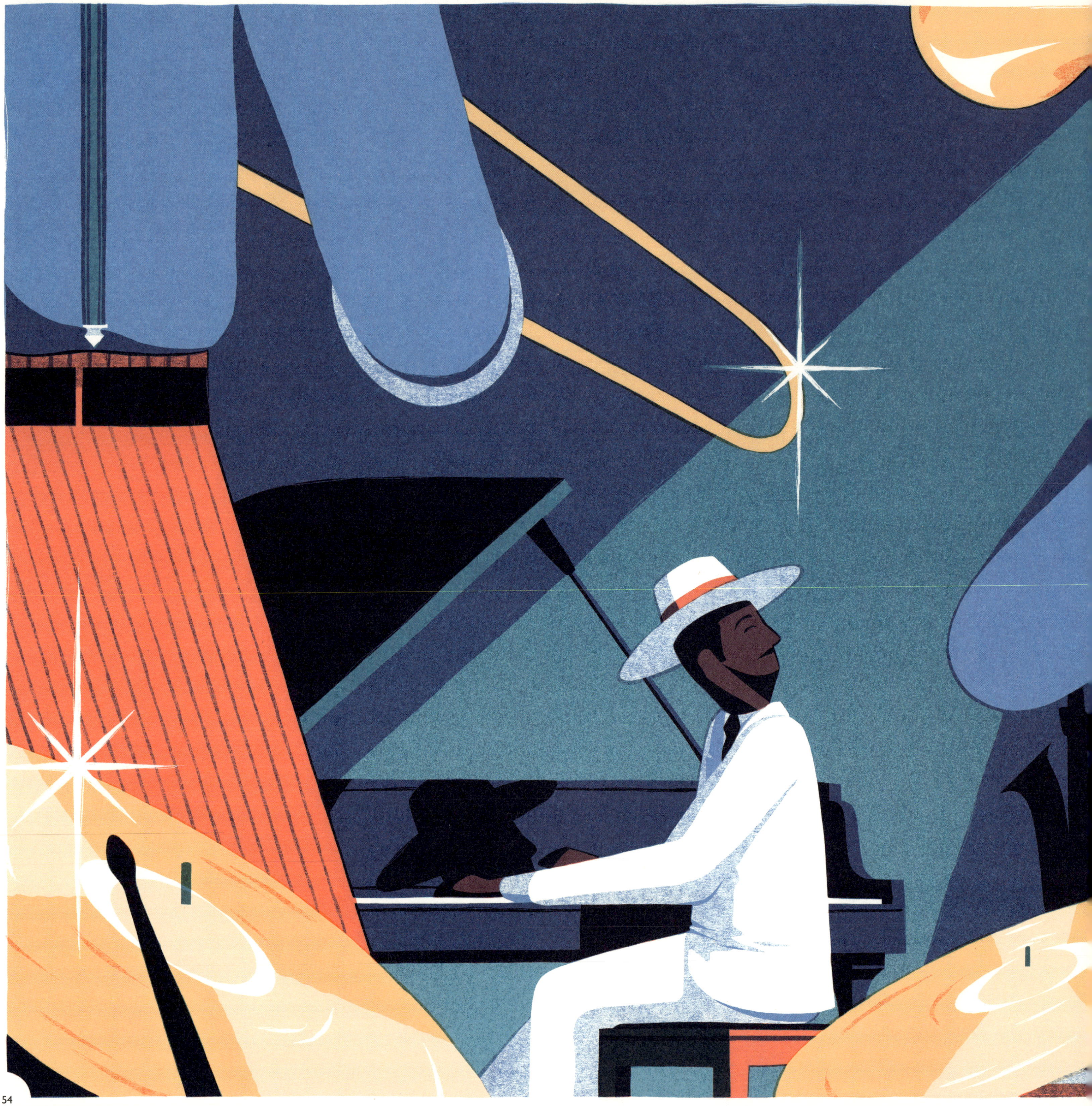

BIG BAND MAESTRO:
DUKE ELLINGTON
(1899–1974)

Edward Kennedy 'Duke' Ellington was an American composer, pianist and bandleader. He is one of the twentieth century's most important jazz composers, creating over two thousand instrumental pieces, from dance and sacred music to popular songs – many of which are still played regularly by jazz musicians around the world!

Ellington's group of hand-picked musicians is often described as a 'jazz orchestra'. The instruments used are totally different to that of a symphony orchestra. It sounds more like a big band, comprising saxophones, clarinet, trumpets, trombones, guitar, piano, bass and drums – with some of the band adding vocals and one trumpet player even doubling on violin!

In a jazz orchestra the musicians are encouraged to include **improvisation**, and so no two performances are ever the same. Ellington selected musicians for their individual ability to improvise as well as their ability to read the parts he'd composed. He wanted musicians who had unique playing styles, so that both the improvised solos and written **ensemble** music would have a personality and energy that no one had quite heard before.

HALL OF FAME

MOZART (1756–1791)

Wolfgang Amadeus Mozart, a famous classical composer who lived nearly 300 years ago, was so naturally gifted that he composed his first symphony when he was just eight years old! He went on to compose some of the most well-known pieces of all time.

BEETHOVEN (1770–1827)

The great classical composer Ludwig van Beethoven started a very important movement in classical music called 'romanticism'. He was so talented that he continued to compose incredible symphonies long after he completely lost his hearing!

MENDELSSOHN (1809–1847)

The extraordinarily talented composer Felix Mendelssohn made his public debut aged nine and composed his first symphony at fifteen. It's no wonder Queen Victoria referred to him at the time as 'the greatest musical genius since Mozart'.

ETHEL SMYTH (1858–1944)

Dame Ethel Smyth was a British composer and political activist. Ethel took a two year break from composing to dedicate herself to the suffragette movement, and her empowering piece *The March of the Women* became their anthem.

WILLIAM GRANT STILL (1895–1978)

William Grant Still wrote 150 works and was the first African American to conduct a major US symphony orchestra. Entitled *Symphony No.1 – Afro-American*, it fused together elements of the traditional orchestra with **blues** rhythms.

MICHEL LEGRAND (1932–2019)

As if being an arranger, conductor and jazz pianist wasn't enough, this legendary French composer also wrote over 250 film soundtracks – so it is very likely you have heard his work somewhere before!

STAGE DOOR

BEYOND THE CONCERT HALL

MYTHOLOGY OF MUSIC

As long as humans have made music, that music has been at the heart of many of their myths and legends. Perhaps this is because a truly gifted musician can create melodies that move us emotionally, and feel a bit like magic!

BIBLICAL SOUNDS

The Hebrew bible tells the story of a man called Joshua, who had led a great army to capture the ancient city of Jericho. According to the story, they brought down Jericho's enormous walls using only the mighty sound of an early trumpet called a *shofar*. This would likely have been made from a ram's horn, and would have sounded a bit like a modern day bugle. The shofar actually makes over 70 appearances in the Bible, highlighting its importance.

MYTHICAL MUSIC

The pan flute is an ancient wind instrument that gets its name from a Greek god called Pan, who had the legs and horns of a goat. According to myth, Pan fell in love with a nymph called Syrinx, who escaped him by turning into a river reed. When the wind blew through the reeds it created a beautiful sound, so Pan cut them at different lengths to make the first pan flute, which he dedicated to his lost love.

MAGIC

In the folklore of Scandinavia, a mysterious, **fiddle**-playing water spirit can be found in rivers. Usually known as the *fossegrim* or the *strömkarlen*, it is said that with the right persuasion, this crafty spirit will teach a mortal its musical secrets. Some say that the greatest Scandinavian violinists learned their skill from this spirit.

OPERA

In an **opera**, performers work together with the orchestra to tell a story. An opera is different from an orchestral performance with a choir because the stage is decorated to create a scene, and the performers are in costume and move around as they would in a play. Because they involve singing, operas use words as well as music to help tell their stories. Classical operas are often performed in their original language, which is usually Italian, French, German or Russian.

Many different styles of singing were developed for the orchestra. Recitative singing is intended to simulate speech, and so it is often sung quickly and with a natural rhythm. An 'aria' is a set piece designed for a soloist, usually without any musical accompaniment, and is intended to express emotion. 'Bel canto' means 'beautiful singing' in Italian. Although hard to describe, these pieces are designed to really show off a singer's range and technique. The experience for the audience can be rich, full and tender all at once.

Carmen, written by Georges Bizet and first performed in 1875, is one of the most important operas in the western **canon**. Its dramatic, emotionally-charged melodies and **libretto** tell the story of the madness of love and jealousy between a Spanish soldier and a provocative woman named Carmen.

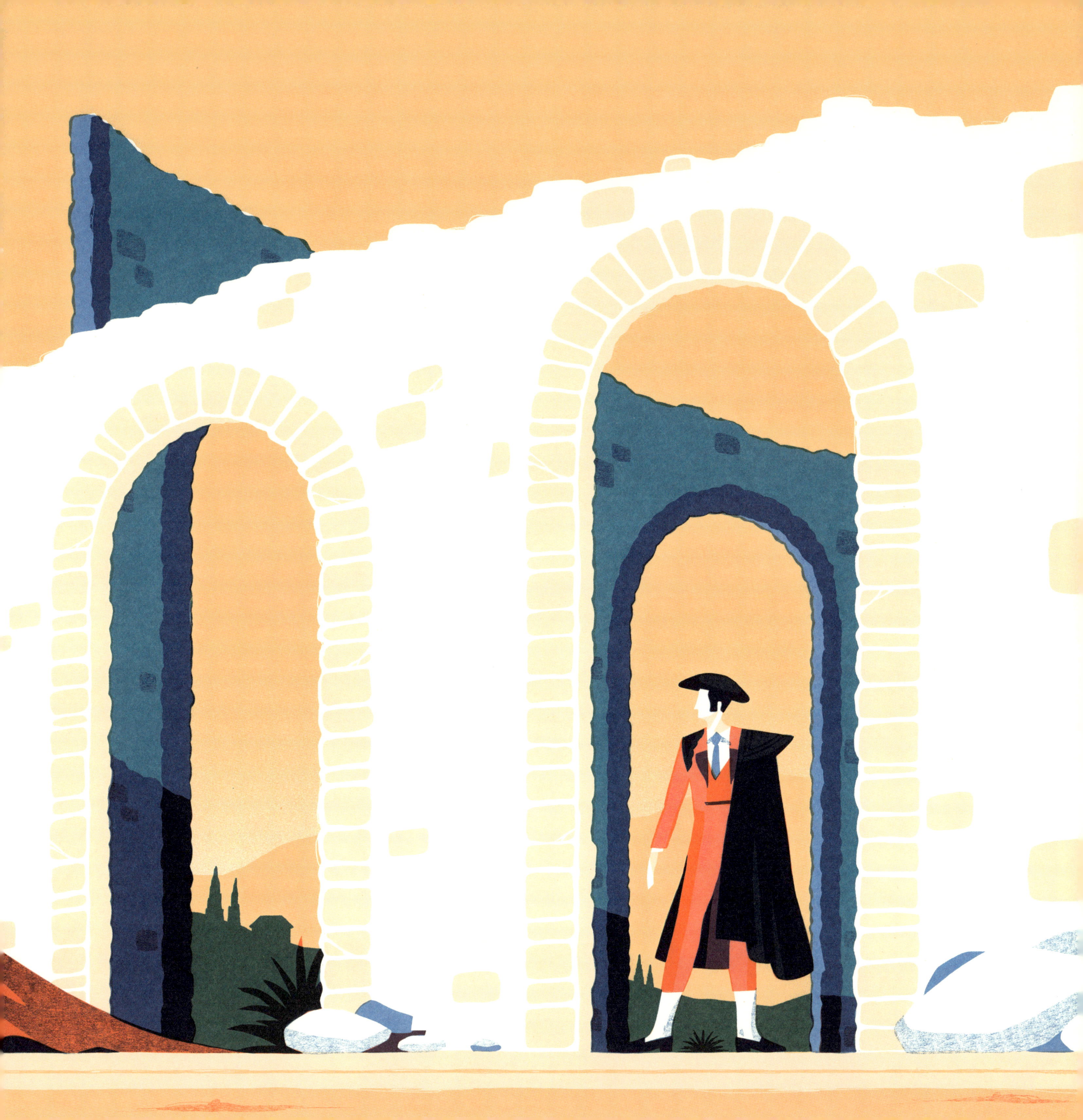

ORCHESTRA AND DANCE

Sometimes it is not lyrics that help an orchestra tell a story, but movement. Ballet is a beautiful centuries-old form of dance that is usually performed to music being played by an orchestra.

In the later part of the nineteenth century, Peter Ilyich Tchaikovsky, a Russian composer, wrote the music for three of the most famous ballets in history: *Swan Lake*, *The Sleeping Beauty*, and perhaps greatest of all, *The Nutcracker*, whose performance has become a winter tradition in some countries. The dreamy music, **choreography**, costumes and set design of these ballets all work together to create some truly captivating performances.

COMPOSING FOR MUSICAL THEATRE

When orchestral music, singing, acting and dancing all come together on a stage, they create **musical theatre**. It takes many people with different skills to create a musical. Like orchestral music, a musical needs a composer to create its music. It also needs a writer to create the story and **dialogue**, a **lyricist** (or *librettist*) to write the words that will be sung and a choreographer to decide how all of the characters will move and dance onstage.

West Side Story, first performed in 1957, is one of the most popular musicals ever written. It is a story set on the upper west side of New York City, U.S., where two young people, each from a rival gang, fall in love. It is a thrilling modern **adaptation** of Shakespeare's famous play, *Romeo and Juliet*. Like any musical, *West Side Story* was a group effort: the story and text are written by Arthur Laurents, with music by Leonard Bernstein, lyrics by Stephen Sondheim and choreography by Jerome Robbins. It was so successful as a **Broadway** musical that it was eventually made into a film!

COMPOSING FOR CINEMA

Even if you've never been to a live performance, it's likely you've heard many different orchestras play – in films! Many have scores which are created by film composers and then performed by an orchestra in a recording studio. Although you cannot see the orchestra playing, their music is designed to capture the feeling of a film and help tell the story.

A film's music must blend well with what is happening on-screen. Sometimes, a film director will give the composer a **storyboard** or script of the movie before it is created, giving the composer the freedom to write based on what they think the film should sound like. Other times, a composer writes and records the score once the film has already been shot and edited; they then use different techniques to **synchronise** their music with what is happening on the screen.

No one has written as many iconic film scores as the American composer John Williams. You will have already heard his work if you have seen any films in the *Star Wars*, *Harry Potter* or *Indiana Jones* series, or other classic blockbusters like *Jurassic Park*, *Jaws* or *E.T. the Extra-Terrestrial*.

ORCHESTRA AND TECHNOLOGY

Digital technology is making its way into more and more parts of our lives, and orchestral music is no exception! New technology has not only changed the way music is performed, but also the way it is written. Today, a composer with a computer and an electronic keyboard can write a piece of music for an entire orchestra and know exactly what it will sound like before it is performed!

Using **sample** recordings of real instruments, a musician can play a digital keyboard and make it sound like almost any instrument – or group of instruments – you can think of. You could press just a couple of keys to create the sound of a violin, a whole woodwind section or even an entire symphony! A composer can experiment with digital samples to explore sounds while writing. Later, these sounds can be performed by a live orchestra.

The theremin is a curious electronic instrument that can occasionally be seen in an orchestra. This unusual machine does not actually need to be touched in order to be played! Its eerie sound is created by radio waves which are **amplified** through a speaker, and the player can control its pitch and volume by moving their hands through the air surrounding the two antennae.

GETTING INVOLVED

It is fascinating to learn about musical instruments and the brilliant music that has been composed for them... but maybe you're ready to start playing some music yourself!

There are many ways to start learning an instrument or writing music. Many schools have music programmes where students can learn to play an instrument and have the experience of playing in a group. You might even be lucky enough to own your own musical instrument, and could form a group of your own.

However you choose to start, the most important thing is to pick up an instrument and start playing… and then, to practice, practice, practice! Playing music with other people is a great way to make new friends, improve your skills, and learn about new music.

Why not try to create your own orchestra?

GLOSSARY

Abbess The leader of a group of Christian nuns, which are religious women who live together and devote their lives to their god.

Accompaniment A musical part that supports, or accompanies another instrument.

Acoustics The study and knowledge of how sound works.

Adaptation A film or play that has been changed from the original written script.

Amplify To make a sound louder.

Audience A group of spectators who attend a performance.

Beat A regular pulse. A beat sets the pace of the music.

Blues A style of African American music, which typically expresses feelings of sadness.

Broadway A famous street in the city of New York where some of America's most famous theatres are found.

Canon The name for a group of musical works that are most famous and highly praised in a particular culture.

Choreography The movements and steps in a dance.

Climax The most exciting or important part of a musical performance.

Concerto A composition (often in three movements) for a solo instrument with an accompanying orchestra.

Consort A group of musicians typically associated with English music during the Renaissance period.

Dialogue A conversation between two or more people.

Dynamics The change in volume of a musical performance.

Electronics To produce sound using electrical currents.

Embouchure The way in which a musician uses their mouth (lips, teeth and tongue) when playing a brass or wind instrument to produce sound.

Engineering The study of engines, machines and structures

Ensemble A group of musicians who perform together.

Fiddle An informal word for a violin, normally associated with traditional folk music.

Flautist A person who plays the flute.

Gregorian chant A type of choral music sung in churches during the medieval period.

Harmony A combination of notes played at the same time to create a sound.

Hollow Having a hole, or empty space inside. This can amplify sound.

Improvisation To make music spontaneously, without the need for a composer to generate a written part for the musician to read from.

Libretto Words that are set to music and sung either as a single song or for an opera or musical.

Lyricist A person who writes lyrics.

Lyrics The words of a song, sung by a singer or choir.

Melody A series of notes played one after the other which create a pleasing tune.

MEMORISE To learn or remember something by heart.

MOVEMENT A smaller, complete section within a larger musical composition.

MUSICAL THEATRE A type of performance that combines acting, singing and dancing.

NOTE A written musical symbol that represents a sound.

OPERA A type of musical drama using songs and music to tell a story.

PERCUSSIONIST A person who plays a percussion instrument.

PIONEER A person who has developed new techniques or ideas.

PITCH The highness or lowness of the sound made by an instrument.

PODIUM A wooden box or platform on which a conductor stands so that they can be easily seen.

POLYMATH A person who knows a great deal about many different subjects.

POROUS Describes a material which has very tiny holes, allowing water to soak through.

PROLIFIC Describes someone who has produced a great many works.

RESONATE To ring and vibrate for a more extended period of time.

RHYTHM The regular, repeated pattern of sounds in a musical piece.

ROSIN A hard and sticky substance made from resin – an organic material produced by some trees.

SAMPLE A small portion of a sound recording.

SIGHT-READ To play music without having seen, prepared or rehearsed the music beforehand.

SOUND WAVE A wave of pressure moving through the air, which we perceive in the form of sound.

STORYBOARD A series of sketches, created in a sequence to visualise scenes in a film.

SUITE A group of movements which follow on from one another.

SYMPHONY A musical composition, meant to be performed by a full orchestra.

SYNCHRONISE When two or more things to occur at the same rate.

TEMPO The speed at which music is played.

TEXTURE A way of describing musical layers. It can refer to harmonies, melodies and tempo.

TUNE To adjust an instrument to the correct pitch.

UNISON To perform all at the same time.

UPTEMPO An increase in the beat of the music so it is played faster.

VALVE An adjustable piece of a brass instrument which changes its pitch when moved.

VIBRATE To make very small and fast movements back and forth.

VIRTUOSO A person with especially strong skills in a particular field, especially music.

VOCAL RANGE The pitches of sound that a person is capable of producing with their voice.

INDEX

Acoustics 36, 38
amplify 16, 20, 24, 28, 29, 31, 38
aria 62
audience 13, 45, 62

Ballet 64-65
bandleader 55
baritone 33
bass (voice) 33
bass drum 27
bassoon 19, 20
baton 13
beat 43, 52
Beach, Amy 51
Beethoven, Ludwig van 56
bel canto 62
Bernstein, Leonard 67
Bizet, Georges 63
Boston 51
bow 14, 17

brass 12, 18, 22, 23, 24, 31, 53
Broadway 67

Canon 63
Carmen 63
castanets 27
cello 14, 15
choir 33, 53, 62
choreography 65, 67
cinema 68
clarinet 19, 20-21, 31, 55
    contrabass 19
    sopranino 19
classical guitar 31
clef 43
concert hall 36, 38
    Wiener Musikverein 38
concerto 44, 48
conductor 12, 13, 44, 57
consorts 11
contralto 33

countertenor 33
crotchet 43
cymbals 27

Digital 70
double bass 15, 19
drum sticks 28
dynamics 44

Elbphilharmonie 36
electronic keyboard 70
Ellington, Duke 55
embouchure 24
ensemble 55
E.T. The Extra-Terrestrial 69

Flautist 20
flute 18, 20, 52
fossegrim 61
The Four Seasons 48-49
French horn 22

Gaelic Symphony 51
glockenspiel 52
Gregorian chants 47

Hansen, Theophil 38
hardwoods 34, 35
    Cocobolo 34
    Ebony 34
    Maple 34
    Pernambuco 34
harmony 27, 33
Harry Potter 69
Hebrew 60
Hildegard of Bingen 47
Holst, Gustav 52-53

Improvisation 55
Indiana Jones 69
Irish folk melodies 51

Jaws 69
jazz 22, 31, 55, 57
Jurassic Park 69

Kettledrum 26
keyboard 30

Laurents, Arthur 67
Legrand, Michel 57
libretto 63
lyricist 66
lyrics 45, 64, 67

Mallet 26, 28, 29
marimba 26
melody 27, 44, 48
Mendelssohn, Felix 56
mezzo-soprano 33
minim 43
movements 48, 49
Mozart, Wolfgang Amadeus 56

musical theatre 66-67
mute 24
   harmon mute 24
mythology 60

Note 14, 17, 19, 21, 25, 26, 28, 29, 43, 53
The Nutcracker 65

Oboe 18, 20
opera 62-63
organ 30, 53

Pan 60
pan flute 60
percussion 12, 26-27, 28, 53
   tuned 25
   untuned 26
percussionist 26
piano 11, 26, 27, 29, 30, 34, 55
pick 3

pitch 14
The Planets 52-53
plectrum 31
podium 13
polymath 47
professional singer 32

Quaver 43

Recitative 62
reed 20, 21, 24, 31, 60
Renaissance 11
rest 43, 44
rhythm 26, 27, 43, 44, 49, 52, 62
Robbins, Jerome 67
Romeo and Juliet 67
Royal Albert Hall 37

Sample 70
saxophone 31
score 44

script 44, 68
semibreve 43
Shakespeare 67
shofar 60
sight-reading 42
The Sleeping Beauty 65
Smyth, Ethel 57
snare drum 27, 28
softwoods 35
   Cedar 35
   Spruce 35
soloists 33, 62
Sondheim, Stephen 67
soprano 33
soundboard 16, 17, 35
sound waves 17
sousaphone 23
Star Wars 69
stave 43
Still, William Grant 57
storyboard 44, 68

strings 12, 14, 16, 17, 28, 29, 52
strömkarlen 61
suite 52
Swan Lake 65
Sydney Opera House 36
symphony 44, 51, 56, 57, 70
symphony orchestra 12, 31, 55, 57

Tchaikovsky, Peter Ilyich 65
tempo 13, 44, 49, 52, 53
tenor 33
theremin 71
timpani 26, 28, 53
trombone 23, 24, 55
trumpet 11, 22, 24-25, 55, 60
tuba 23
tube 22, 24, 25, 29

Unison 33

Valves 24
vibraphone 26, 29
vibration 16, 21, 24, 28, 35
viola 14, 15, 34
violin 11, 14, 16, 17, 48, 55, 70
   first violins 14
   leader 14
   second violins 14
Vivaldi, Antonio 48-49
vocal chords 32
vocal range 33

West Side Story 67
Williams, John 69
woodwind 12, 18, 19, 20, 22, 24, 31, 70

Xylophone 26, 29